gr 2-3

23.95

BUFFALO
BILLS

by Tom Robinson

Published by ABDO Publishing Company, 8000 West 78th Street, Edina, Minnesota 55439. Copyright © 2011 by Abdo Consulting Group, Inc. International copyrights reserved in all countries. No part of this book may be reproduced in any form without written permission from the publisher. SportsZone™ is a trademark and logo of ABDO Publishing Company.

Printed in the United States of America,
North Mankato, Minnesota
062010
092010

 THIS BOOK CONTAINS AT LEAST 10% RECYCLED MATERIALS.

Editor: Chrös McDougall
Copy Editor: Nicholas Cafarelli
Interior Design and Production: Christa Schneider
Cover Design: Christa Schneider

Photo Credits: Dean Duprey/AP Images, cover; NFL Photos/AP Images, 1, 7, 12, 25, 26, 31, 42 (top), 42 (bottom); Lennox McLendon/AP Images, 4; Paul Spinelli/AP Images, 8, 37; Chris O'Meara/AP Images, 11, 43 (top); AP Images, 14, 16, 20, 23, 29, 42 (middle); Ed Kolenovsky/AP Images, 19; Diamond Images/Getty Images, 33; Doug Mills/AP Images, 34, 43 (middle); Mike Groll/AP Images, 39, 44; Maria Lavendier/AP Images, 41, 43 (bottom); David Duprey/AP Images, 47

Library of Congress Cataloging-in-Publication Data
Robinson, Tom. 1964-
  Buffalo Bills / Tom Robinson.
    p. cm. — (Inside the NFL)
  Includes index.
  ISBN 978-1-61714-004-4
  1. Buffalo Bills (Football team)—History—Juvenile literature. I. Title.
  GV956.B83J37 2011
  796.332'640974797—dc22
                                        2010013672

TABLE OF CONTENTS

CHAPTER 1

SUPER CLOSE

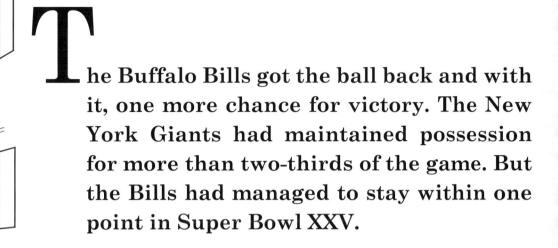

The Buffalo Bills got the ball back and with it, one more chance for victory. The New York Giants had maintained possession for more than two-thirds of the game. But the Bills had managed to stay within one point in Super Bowl XXV.

It was January 27, 1991. The Bills had a chance of winning in their first Super Bowl appearance, which was in Tampa, Florida. There was only 2:16 left. The score was 20–19. Now the game was in the hands of Bills star quarterback Jim Kelly and running back Thurman Thomas. If the Bills could get a score, the team would likely win.

STELLAR SEASON

The Buffalo Bills had a standout 1990 regular season. Their 13–3 record was the best in the American Football Conference (AFC). The team's 428 total points were the most in the NFL. That offense was led by star quarterback Jim Kelly. He was the highest-rated passer in the league that season. In the two play-off games before the Super Bowl, Kelly hit 36 of 52 passes for 639 yards and five touchdowns.

BILLS QUARTERBACK JIM KELLY CELEBRATES AFTER PASSING FOR BUFFALO'S FIRST TOUCHDOWN IN SUPER BOWL XXV.

JIM KELLY

The Buffalo Bills drafted quarterback Jim Kelly in the first round of the 1983 NFL Draft. But Kelly decided that he did not want to play with the struggling team. Instead, he joined the Houston Gamblers of the United States Football League (USFL). He was one of the league's biggest stars until it folded two years later.

With the Gamblers gone, Kelly reported to the Buffalo Bills in 1986. There, he ran coach Marv Levy's no-huddle offense. At the time, he became the fourth-fastest player to pass for 30,000 yards. Kelly worked with star running back Thurman Thomas and star wide receiver Andre Reed. Kelly led the Bills to the playoffs eight times during his 11 seasons with the team. He was inducted into the Pro Football Hall of Fame in 2002.

Buffalo began from its own 10-yard line. Kelly stepped behind the center and began to run the two-minute-drill offense. Teams take that approach when they need to score quickly. Kelly and the offense began steadily moving up the field. Behind runs of 22 and 11 yards by Thomas, the Bills had moved to New York's 29-yard line in just seven plays.

The Bills had used up their final timeout along the way. So on the next play, Kelly spiked the ball into the ground to stop the clock. Only eight seconds remained.

Buffalo's fate was turned to kicker Scott Norwood. Adding the 10 yards of the end zone and almost eight yards between the center and the holder, Norwood was faced with a 47-yard field goal attempt. If he made it, Buffalo would win.

BUFFALO RUNNING BACK THURMAN THOMAS RUNS 31 YARDS TOWARD THE END ZONE IN THE FOURTH QUARTER OF SUPER BOWL XXV.

Norwood could have been a Super Bowl hero. But there was no guarantee that he would make it. From that distance, National Football League (NFL) kickers miss more field goals than they make. Norwood himself had a season-best of 48 yards.

The pressure was on. Some players on each sideline knelt in prayer. Others held hands. Some simply looked away.

Buffalo holder Frank Reich received the snap cleanly. He placed the ball on the field. Then

Norwood blasted it with his right foot. The kicker made solid contact with the ball. After his follow-through, Norwood raised his head to watch.

Millions of people around the United States watched the ball as it sailed through the air. None had a better view than Norwood himself. "By that time," Norwood said, "I knew the kick wasn't good." He was right. The

ball had enough distance, but it floated just inches wide of the right goalpost.

Looking back, Norwood believed he did almost everything right on the kick. Almost. "I wanted to hit the ball solid and I did," he said in a postgame interview. "I wanted to get the kick off fast and I wanted to get it high, so it wouldn't be blocked. And I did. I just didn't get my hips into it enough."

Those few inches would come back to haunt Bills fans. The team reached the Super Bowl in each of the next three years but lost all three. Buffalo became the only team in NFL history to lose four straight Super Bowls. As of 2010, Buffalo had never been closer to a Super Bowl victory than those few inches.

MARV LEVY

Marv Levy took over as coach of the Buffalo Bills in 1986. He brought with him a complex, no-huddle offense. Levy's style helped showcase quarterback Jim Kelly and the team's other talented skill-position players. The coach turned around a struggling team. They went from a losing record to a 10-year stretch in which the Bills had the best record in the AFC. The Harvard-educated coach was inducted into the Pro Football Hall of Fame in 2001.

SCOTT NORWOOD'S KICK SAILED WIDE RIGHT AS BUFFALO LOST TO THE NEW YORK GIANTS 20–19 IN SUPER BOWL XXV.

THE REICH STUFF

As quarterback for the University of Maryland, Frank Reich led one of the biggest comebacks in college football history. Maryland was losing 31–0 to the University of Miami. But Maryland ended up winning 42–40.

Reich had another opportunity for a comeback with the Bills during a 1993 playoff game. With starter Jim Kelly injured, Reich filled in at quarterback. The Bills were down 35–3 to the Houston Oilers with 13:19 left in the third quarter.

The Bills' comeback began when Kenneth Davis scored on a 1-yard rush. Reich then threw three touchdown passes—all before the quarter was over. Reich added another touchdown in the fourth quarter. The teams were tied after regulation. Then Bills kicker Steve Christie hit a 32-yard field goal in overtime for the 41–38 victory.

The Bills next-closest attempt came the following year, after the 1991 season. The Washington Redskins opened up a 24–0 lead. Buffalo charged back in the third quarter. It was not enough. On a day in which Kelly threw four interceptions, Buffalo lost 37–24.

The next two attempts were not as close. Quarterback Troy Aikman led the Dallas Cowboys to a 52–17 rout over the Bills in Super Bowl XXVII. The same teams met again at Super Bowl XXVIII. The Bills took a 13–6 lead into halftime. But Dallas roared back behind running back Emmitt Smith's two touchdowns to win 30–13.

Bills fans are still waiting to forget about those few inches.

SCOTT NORWOOD WALKS OFF THE FIELD AFTER MISSING THE 47-YARD FIELD GOAL THAT WOULD HAVE WON SUPER BOWL XXV.

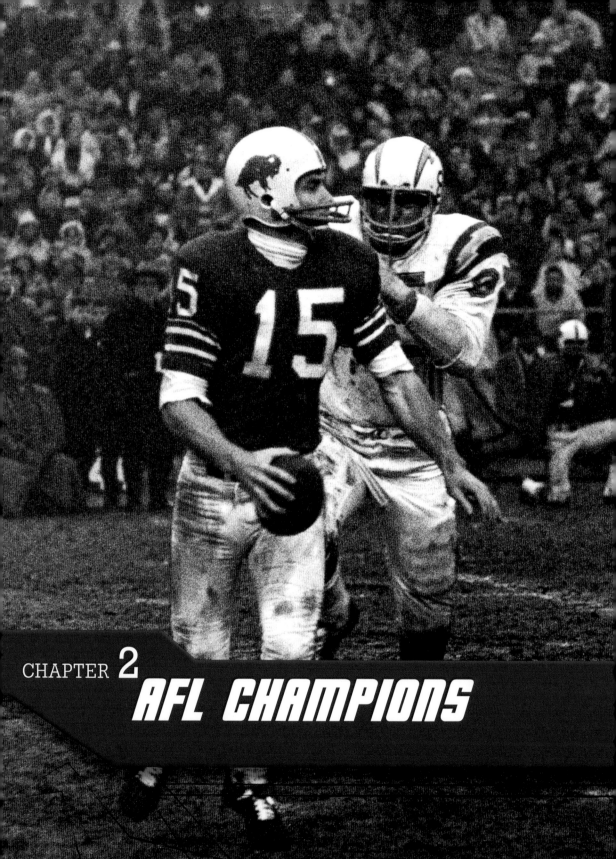

CHAPTER 2
AFL CHAMPIONS

The American Football League (AFL) awarded six charter franchises in 1959. They were the Dallas Texans, Houston Oilers, New York Titans, Denver Broncos, Los Angeles Chargers, and a Minnesota team. Before the first game, Minnesota instead became the Oakland Raiders. The Buffalo Bills and Boston Patriots were also added that fall. The league would have eight teams for its first season in 1960.

Ralph Wilson Jr. was the owner of the Buffalo Bills. Buster Ramsey was the Bills' first coach. The team began with a 27–3 loss to the New York Titans on September 11, 1960. They had a season-low 113 yards of total offense in the game.

The Bills' first win came 12 days later. They went on the road to beat the Patriots 13–0. The Bills forced seven turnovers in the win. After four seasons, the team had still not won more than half of its games. But that was to change in 1964.

JACK KEMP LOOKS FOR AN OPEN RECEIVER DURING THE BILLS' 20–7 WIN OVER THE SAN DIEGO CHARGERS IN THE 1964 AFL CHAMPIONSHIP GAME.

The groundwork for the change had begun two seasons earlier. The team hired Lou Saban as coach in 1962. After losing their first five games, the Bills finished 7–6–1 that season. Jack Kemp took over as quarterback the next season. The Bills started 0–3–1. After adjusting to the new quarterback, they finished the last 10 games 7–3. Buffalo had defeated the New York Jets in back-to-back games at the end of that season. With a 7–6–1 record, the Bills were tied for the East division title. They faced the Boston Patriots in a playoff. However, they lost 26–8.

In 1964, the Bills wasted no time getting hot. This time, they won their first nine games.

BILLS OWNER RALPH WILSON JR., *BACK ROW, CENTER*, POSES WITH REPRESENTATIVES FROM THE OTHER AFL TEAMS IN 1959.

RALPH WILSON JR.

As of 2010, Ralph Wilson Jr. was the only owner the Buffalo Bills had ever had. He was also one of the men most responsible for merging the AFL and the NFL before the 1970 season. In 1997, the NFL Alumni Association awarded Wilson with the "Order of the Leather Helmet." The honor is given to people who have made "substantial contributions to professional football." Wilson was inducted into the Pro Football Hall of Fame in 2009.

Wilson owned part of the NFL's Detroit Lions before the Buffalo Bills existed. Then, in 1959, he joined with six other AFL owners and created the Bills before the league's first season. He later became president of the AFL. Few believed the AFL would succeed, but Wilson played a big role in making sure it did. In 1965, he began talks that led to the AFL–NFL merger. After that, Wilson remained active in behind-the-scenes operations for the league.

COACH LOU SABAN, *LEFT*, CHEERS WITH PETE GOGOLAK (3), JACK KEMP (15), AND WRAY CARLTON (30) AFTER THE 1964 AFL CHAMPIONSHIP GAME.

WHAT'S IN A NAME?

The Buffalo Bills were named after Buffalo Bill Cody. He was a famous Western frontiersman during the 1800s. In 1946, the Buffalo Bisons joined the All-America Football Conference. The team changed its name to the Buffalo Bills in 1947. It kept the name until it broke up in 1949. When Ralph Wilson Jr. bought the AFL franchise in 1959, he decided to honor the former team's name.

Only then did they lose their first game 36–28 to Boston. In their fifth game, Kemp led the team to a record offensive performance against the Houston Oilers. He completed 14 of 26 passes for 378 yards and three touchdowns. Receiver Elbert Dubenion caught five passes for 183 yards and a touchdown. Receiver Glenn Bass caught five passes for 147 yards and two touchdowns. The Bills won 48–17. It was the first time in franchise history that the offense had racked up more than 500 yards.

Buffalo's 12–2 record was easily the best in the AFL that year. The Bills met the San Diego Chargers in the AFL Championship Game. It was Kemp's chance for payback. He had led the Chargers to the 1960 and 1961 championship games. Then, in 1962, Kemp was injured. The Chargers placed him on waivers, allowing any team to sign him. The Bills did just that.

San Diego scored the first time it had the ball. But the Chargers were shut down by the Buffalo defense the rest of the way. The Bills defeated the Chargers 20–7. Kemp completed 10 of 20 passes for 188 yards. Running back Cookie Gilchrist rushed for 122 yards on 16 carries. He had led the AFL in rushing during the 1962 and 1964 seasons. However, the AFL Championship would be his last game with the Bills.

The Bills had another strong start in 1965. They won six of their first seven games and finished 10–3–1. The AFL Championship Game was a rematch from the year before. The West champion Chargers had beaten and tied the Bills in the regular season.

Buffalo's defense had allowed the fewest points in the league during the season. With Gilchrist gone and Dubenion and Bass injured, the Bills needed a strong performance from the defense.

In the AFL Championship, the defense outscored San Diego by itself. Butch Byrd returned an interception 74 yards for a score. Ernie Warlick scored on a touchdown pass from Kemp, and Pete Gogolak converted three field goals. Buffalo ended up winning 23–0.

"This is the only club we didn't beat this year," Saban said of the San Diego Chargers. "And, of course, we wanted this one real bad."

BUFFALO RUNNING BACK ROGER KOCHMAN TRIES TO BREAK THROUGH THE LINE DURING A 1963 GAME IN HOUSTON.

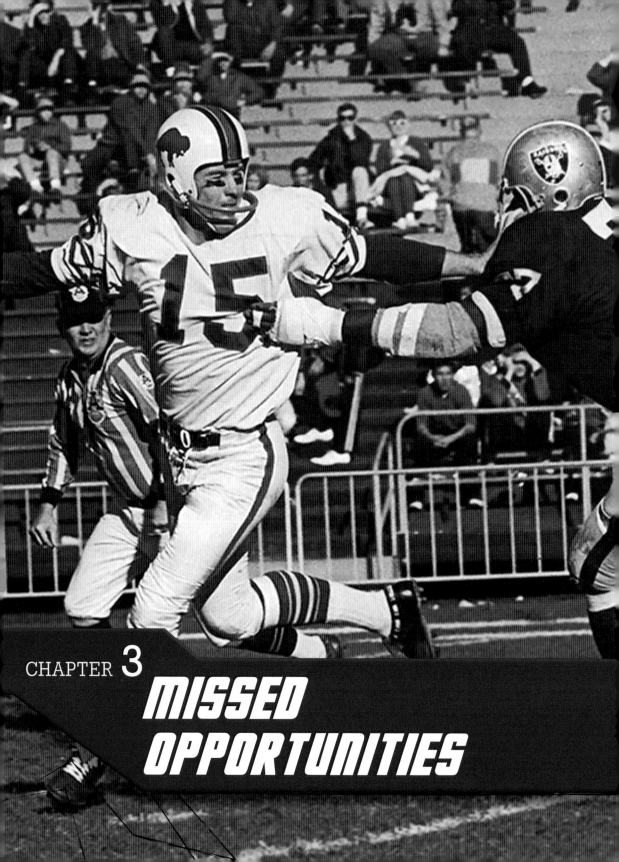

CHAPTER 3

MISSED OPPORTUNITIES

The 1966 AFL season quickly became an important one. Buffalo Bills owner Ralph Wilson Jr. was leading the way as the AFL began working with the more-established National Football League (NFL). The champions of the two leagues would meet at the end of the season in the first AFL-NFL world championship game. This would eventually become known as the Super Bowl.

As two-time defending AFL champions, Buffalo was a popular pick to play in the first Super Bowl. But the Bills nearly missed the entire AFL playoffs. They won six of their last seven games to finish 9–4–1 and barely make the playoffs.

The AFL West champion Kansas City Chiefs came to Buffalo for the first round of the playoffs. With a win, the Bills would have a shot at their third straight AFL title. They would also have a shot to play in the first Super Bowl.

BILLS QUARTERBACK JACK KEMP TRIES TO AVOID BEING TACKLED BY AN OAKLAND RAIDER DURING A 1967 GAME.

Trouble started for the Bills when they fumbled on the opening kickoff. That set up an early Kansas City touchdown. The Bills came right back when Jack Kemp threw a 69-yard touchdown pass to Elbert Dubenion. But Buffalo did not score again. Down 14–7, the Bills reached the Kansas City 10-yard line. But Johnny Robinson intercepted a pass and returned it 72 yards. That set up a Mike Mercer field goal that gave the Chiefs a 17–7 halftime lead. Mike Garrett added two second-half touchdowns for Kansas City. The Chiefs pulled away for the 31–7 win. Buffalo had four turnovers in the game.

After those three strong seasons, the Bills began to struggle. During the 1967–71 seasons, Buffalo posted a combined 13–55–2 record. The team won just once a month in 1967. It even had two seasons where it won just once each season.

Buffalo twice came close to a winless season. The team's only win during the 1968 season came against the New York Jets. Even so, the Jets had 427 yards of offense to Buffalo's 197.

AFL ALL-TIME TEAM

The Pro Football Hall of Fame announced the AFL All-Time Team in January 1970. The Bills had three players who were first-team selections. They were guard Billy Shaw, defensive tackle Tom Sestak, and safety George Saimes. Tackle Stew Barber, linebacker Mike Stratton, and cornerback Butch Byrd were picked for the second team. The second team also included four players who spent time with the Bills and other teams. They were running back Cookie Gilchrist, wide receiver Art Powell, defensive end Ron McDole, and defensive tackle Tom Keating.

BILLS SAFETY HAGOOD CLARKE BREAKS UP A PASS INTENDED FOR BOSTON PATRIOTS RECEIVER JIM WHALEN IN A 1968 GAME.

BILLY SHAW

Billy Shaw was the first player to spend his entire career in the AFL and be named to the Pro Football Hall of Fame. Although the Dallas Cowboys of the NFL had drafted him, Shaw decided to join the Buffalo Bills in 1961. He felt like his skills would be better used by the Bills.

After playing offense and defense at Georgia Tech, he settled in as offensive guard in Buffalo. Shaw was one of the leaders of a strong running game that gave the Bills a different look from many teams in the AFL. The league was known for its wide-open passing games. The Bills teams of the early 1960s rank as some of the top-scoring running teams in franchise history.

Shaw was a first-team AFL all-star for five consecutive seasons from 1962–66. He was a second-team choice three other times. He was a member of both the All-Time AFL Team and pro football's All-Decade Team of the 1960s.

The Bills beat the Jets by forcing six turnovers, four of them interceptions. Tom Janik returned one of those interceptions 100 yards for a second-quarter touchdown. Butch Byrd and Booker Edgerson each returned interceptions for touchdowns in the fourth quarter.

The 1971 Bills went winless into the final weekend in November. Dennis Shaw threw touchdown passes of 11 and 47 yards to J. D. Hill. Buffalo ended up beating the New England Patriots 27–20.

While the Bills struggled on the field, they were making a transition off it. Along with nine other AFL teams, Buffalo joined the NFL in 1970.

The Bills joined AFL East rivals New York Jets, Patriots, and Miami Dolphins in the

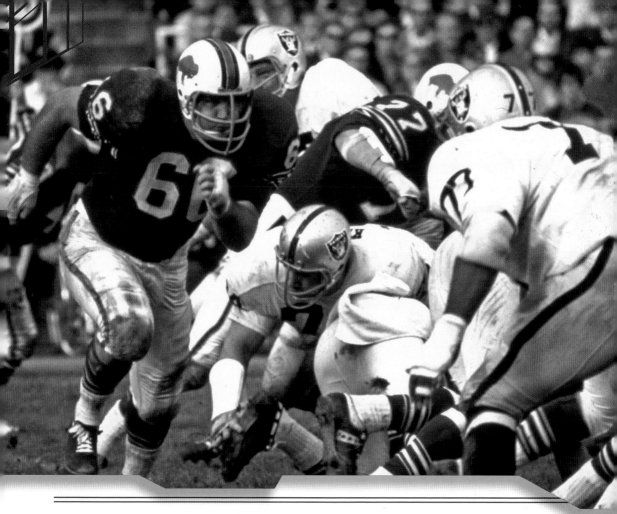

BILLY SHAW PULLS OUT TO BLOCK IN A 1967 GAME AGAINST THE OAKLAND RAIDERS. HE WENT ON TO ENTER THE PRO FOOTBALL HALL OF FAME.

EXTENDED STRUGGLES

The Buffalo Bills won just once in 22 games from midway through the 1970 season to early in the 1972 season. Buffalo went 0–6–1 in the second half of 1970. It went 1–13 in 1971 and then lost the 1972 season opener. The drought ended with a 27–20 win over the San Francisco 49ers.

American Football Conference (AFC) East division. The Baltimore Colts, who were from the NFL, rounded out the division. They began playing as a unified league in the fall of 1970.

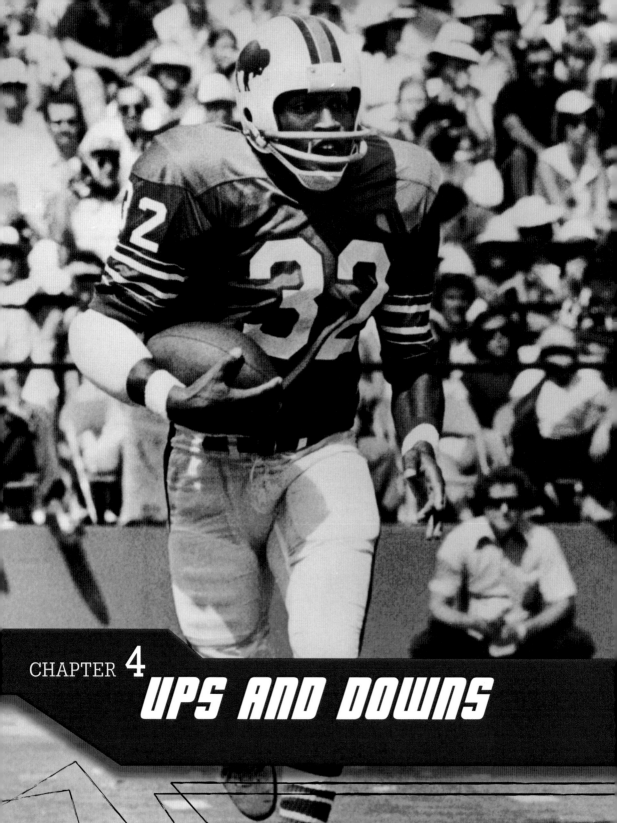

CHAPTER 4

UPS AND DOWNS

Throughout their history, the Buffalo Bills have had extended stretches of success and disappointment. After their five-year slump at the end of the 1960s and early 1970s, the Bills began to improve. That was largely due to the return of coach Lou Saban and the emergence of running back O. J. Simpson.

Simpson ran for 1,251 yards in 1972. That was also Saban's first season back as coach. The 1972 season was the first of Simpson's five straight years of rushing for more than 1,000 yards. The Bills improved from 1–13 in 1971 to 4–9–1 in 1972. In Saban's time as a head coach, that was the only full season in which he had a losing record. But the Bills were soon back to their successful ways. They followed that season with three straight winning seasons.

Joe Ferguson took over as quarterback in 1973. It was the first of his 12 straight seasons

O. J. SIMPSON LOOKS FOR SPACE TO RUN DURING A 1973 GAME. SIMPSON BROKE JIM BROWN'S SINGLE-SEASON RUSHING RECORD THAT SEASON.

MILESTONE MAN

The game was stopped, but the celebration was low key. O. J. Simpson was being recognized for breaking Jim Brown's single-season rushing record early in the final game of the 1973 season.

But there was still more work to be done.

In a win against the New England Patriots, Simpson carried the ball 22 times for 219 yards. In the next game, he carried the ball 34 times for 200 yards in a win over the New York Jets. No other runner had ever produced back-to-back 200-yard games and three such games in the same season.

Simpson's last run against the Jets was more important for a different record. His 7-yard run had made him the first player to rush for more than 2,000 yards in a season. This time, the celebration was more enthusiastic. Simpson's teammates carried him on their shoulders. He finished his season with 2,003 yards.

as starting quarterback. The emphasis in Buffalo, however, remained on the running back. Simpson became the first 2,000-yard rusher in NFL history. He led the Bills to a season-ending, four-game winning streak and a 9–5 record.

Simpson's rushing numbers steeply dropped in 1974. But Ferguson's passing production was on the rise. The Bills started the season 7–1, enough to get them headed toward the playoffs. By the time they arrived at the postseason with a 9–5 record, however, they were struggling. The Pittsburgh Steelers ruined Buffalo's first playoff appearance in eight years. It was also Buffalo's first playoff appearance as a member of the NFL. Pittsburgh's "Steel Curtain" defense held Simpson to 49 rushing yards in the 32–14 loss.

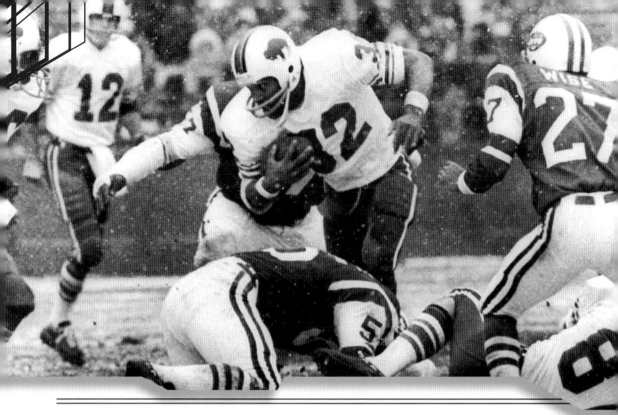

O. J. SIMPSON BURSTS THROUGH THE NEW YORK JETS' DEFENSIVE LINE TO SET THE NFL SEASON RUSHING RECORD IN 1973.

Buffalo's offense peaked during the 1975 season. Simpson bounced back from 1,125 yards rushing in 1974 to 1,817 yards in 1975. Meanwhile, Ferguson nearly doubled his production to 2,426 passing yards and 25 touchdowns. As a result, the Bills led the NFL in scoring with an average of 30 points per game. That would not be enough, though. The Bills started the

2,000-YARD CLUB

Buffalo's O. J. Simpson was the only player to rush for 2,000 yards in a season when the NFL had a 14-game schedule. He rushed 332 times for 2,003 yards and 12 touchdowns in 1973. Five players have run for more than 2,000 yards in a 16-game season. Eric Dickerson ran for a record 2,105 yards for the Los Angeles Rams in 1984. Detroit's Barry Sanders ran for 2,053 in 1997. Then Denver's Terrell Davis ran for 2,008 the next year. Jamal Lewis of the Baltimore Ravens gained 2,066 in 2003. Tennessee's Chris Johnson rushed for 2,006 in 2009.

ELECTRIC COMPANY

A good running back often has a good offensive line. O. J. Simpson was no exception. Joe DeLamielleure and Reggie McKenzie led the Bills' offensive line during Simpson's time in Buffalo. Simpson was nicknamed "Juice." The line earned a nickname of its own: "Electric Company." That was because it "turned the Juice loose." Juice was a slang term for electricity.

DeLamielleure was a first- or second-team All-Pro eight times. After playing seven seasons with the Bills, he spent five years in Cleveland. He completed his career with one more year in Buffalo. He was selected to the NFL's All-Decade Team for the 1970s. In 2003, he was inducted into the Pro Football Hall of Fame.

McKenzie was first-team All-Pro in 1973, Simpson's 2,000-yard season. McKenzie was second-team All-Pro the following two seasons.

season with four straight wins. They fell short of the playoffs, however, with an 8–6 finish.

Saban left the team after a 2–3 start in 1976. He quit when the team stripped him of some of his responsibilities. The players seemed to miss him. Under new coach Jim Ringo, the Bills lost the rest of their nine games in 1976.

Buffalo's ups and downs continued. Under Coach Ringo, the Bills also had a losing season in 1977. When coach Chuck Knox took over in 1978, he had a losing season that year and the next. But then he led the team into the 1980 and 1981 playoffs. After that, however, the Bills went six more years without a winning season.

BILLS QUARTERBACK JOE FERGUSON LOOKS FOR A RECEIVER IN A 1981 GAME IN CINCINNATI.

The 1980 team finished 11–5. The offense was led by all-purpose running back Joe Cribbs. He ran for 1,185 yards and caught 52 passes. The Bills' defense allowed the fewest yards in the league. Buffalo faced the San Diego Chargers in their return to the playoffs. The Bills had a 14–3 lead at halftime. But Ferguson threw three interceptions for the Bills. Chargers quarterback Dan Fouts threw for two second-half touchdowns to give San Diego the 20–14 win.

TARNISHED IMAGE

O. J. Simpson had been a record-setting running back and later a sports broadcaster and actor. But in 1994, he became known for something else. Simpson was charged with the murder of his former wife and her friend. He was found not guilty in 1995. In 2008, Simpson was sent to jail after a jury found him guilty of armed robbery, kidnapping, and other charges. He was sentenced to 33 years.

Ferguson had a career-high 3,652 yards passing in 1981. Cribbs also had 1,000 rushing yards that year, while Frank Lewis had 1,000 receiving yards. A late surge helped the Bills finish 10–6 and claim a wild-card berth. The Bills took a 24–0 lead against the New York Jets in their first playoff game. They went on to win 31–27. Lewis caught seven passes for 158 yards, including two touchdowns. Their playoff run ended the next week. The Cincinnati Bengals beat the Bills 28–21.

The Bills had back-to-back 2–14 seasons in 1984 and 1985. Things began to look better in 1986. Quarterback Jim Kelly joined the team before the season. Then, coach Marv Levy took over mid-season.

QUARTERBACK JIM KELLY HELPED TURN THE BILLS INTO SUPER BOWL CONTENDERS SOON AFTER JOINING THE TEAM IN 1986.

CHAPTER 5

SUSTAINED EXCELLENCE

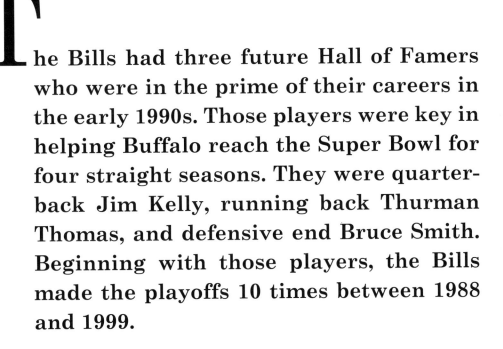

The Bills had three future Hall of Famers who were in the prime of their careers in the early 1990s. Those players were key in helping Buffalo reach the Super Bowl for four straight seasons. They were quarterback Jim Kelly, running back Thurman Thomas, and defensive end Bruce Smith. Beginning with those players, the Bills made the playoffs 10 times between 1988 and 1999.

After six seasons without a winning record, the Bills started 11–1 in 1988, ending up at 12–4. In the playoffs, Thomas ran 11 yards for a touchdown that helped defeat the Houston Oilers 17–10. It was the Bills' first playoff game in seven years.

OLD RIVALS

The Bills have beaten the New York Jets more than they have beaten any other team. The Jets used to be named the Titans. The Bills have lost to the New England Patriots more than they have lost to any other team. The New England team used to be called the Boston Patriots. As of 2009, the Bills were 53–45 against New York and 40–58–1 against the Patriots.

RUNNING BACK THURMAN THOMAS RUNS WITH THE BALL DURING THE BILLS' 1991 PLAYOFF GAME AGAINST THE MIAMI DOLPHINS. BUFFALO WON 44–34.

The luck ran out there, however. Cincinnati stopped Buffalo 21–10 in the AFC Championship.

Kelly, Thomas, and Andre Reed led an explosive offense that helped get the Bills back to the playoffs in 1989. The defense was not as powerful that year, however. Against the Cleveland Browns in the playoffs, Kelly passed for 405 yards and four touchdowns. But the Bills still lost 34–30.

After the loss to the Browns, the Bills won 10 straight AFC playoff games. Those led to the four straight Super Bowl appearances. However, the Bills missed the playoffs following the 1994 season. They returned to the playoffs after the 1995 season. The playoff streak lasted until 1995. They lost 40–21 to

PLAYOFF STREAK

From 1990 until 1995, the Buffalo Bills did not lose an AFC playoff game. During that time, they won 10 games. Their most frequent opponent was the Miami Dolphins, whom they faced in 1990, 1992, and 1995. The biggest win was a 51–3 victory over the Los Angeles Raiders in 1990. The Bills' closest result was a three-point win, which happened twice. In 1991, the Bills beat Denver 10–7. In 1992, the Bills beat the Houston Oilers 41–38 in overtime after trailing 35–3. The Bills outscored opponents 332–167 during those games.

the Pittsburgh Steelers in a divisional playoff game to end the streak.

Thomas had the last of his 1,000-yard rushing seasons in 1996. The aging Bills had enough left to win 10 games that season. They even had a fourth-quarter lead in the playoffs after a 38-yard interception return for a touchdown. But the Jacksonville Jaguars scored the final 10

DEFENSIVE END BRUCE SMITH CELEBRATES AFTER MAKING A PLAY AGAINST THE DETROIT LIONS IN 1997.

BRUCE SMITH

Defensive end Bruce Smith set an NFL record with 200 sacks. He made the NFL's All-Decade Team for both the 1980s and 1990s. Smith was very fast when rushing the passer. This made him a target of double-teams and even triple-teams as opponents tried to keep him from disrupting their offenses.

Smith played for the Buffalo Bills from 1985 to 1999 and the Washington Redskins from 2000 to 2003. The All-American from Virginia Tech lived up to expectations as the first player selected in the 1985 NFL Draft. He was named AFC Defensive Rookie of the Year before twice being named NFL Defensive Player of the Year. He was honored a total of four times as the top defensive player in the AFC. Smith also gave the Bills a 12–3 lead in Super Bowl XXV. He sacked New York Giants quarterback Jeff Hostetler in the end zone for a safety.

points of the wild-card-round game and pulled out a 30–27 victory.

Kelly retired after the 1996 season. A year later, Smith had his last of eight first-team All-Pro seasons. Reed ended a 10-year stretch in which he led the team in receiving nine times. The faces in Buffalo were beginning to change.

With Doug Flutie at quarterback, Buffalo got back to the playoffs after the 1998 and 1999 seasons. But the Bills suffered two painful losses. In 1998, the Bills played the Miami Dolphins in the wild-card round of the playoffs. Flutie passed for 360 yards in the game. Wide receiver Eric Moulds caught nine passes for 240 yards. But the Bills lost 24–17.

The 1999 Bills won seven of their final nine games to reach

BILLS WIDE RECEIVER ERIC MOULDS OUTRUNS THE MIAMI DOLPHINS'
DEFENSE FOR A TOUCHDOWN IN 1999.

the playoffs again. They played the Tennessee Titans. In his last game with the team, Smith had 2.5 sacks. The Bills appeared to have won the game. But then the "Music City Miracle" happened. The Bills kicked off with only a few seconds remaining in the game. On the return, the Titans' Kevin Dyson took a lateral 75 yards for the winning score. Only three seconds remained after that, and the Titans won 22–16.

Moulds caught 94 passes for 1,326 yards in 2000. That helped keep the team in the playoff race. But the Bills followed a four-game winning streak with a four-game losing streak. They finished 8–8. Buffalo lost 10 of its first 11 games the next year.

Quarterback Drew Bledsoe and Moulds formed one of the league's most effective passing combinations in 2002. But the team still finished with only a .500 record. The 2004 team used a late six-game winning streak to go 9–7. That was Buffalo's only winning record from 2000 through 2009.

THURMAN THOMAS

Thurman Thomas was a big part of the Buffalo Bills' high-powered, no-huddle offense. That was because of his combination of pass-catching and running abilities. He led the league in total yards of offense for four straight seasons. When he retired, Thomas ranked ninth in the NFL in rushing with 12,074 yards. He had another 4,458 yards on 472 receptions. Thomas scored 88 touchdowns in his 13-year career. The former Oklahoma State All-American was inducted into the Pro Football Hall of Fame in 2007.

The team had replaced many of its veterans with younger players during the early part of the decade. But the Bills failed to take off behind young quarterback J. P. Losman and running back Willis McGahee, among others. Five straight losing seasons through 2009 left Buffalo tied with the Detroit Lions for the longest active streak without a playoff appearance.

The Bills began a new era in 2008, when they began playing one home game each year in nearby Toronto, Canada. They hoped to begin another new era in 2010, when they hired former Dallas Cowboys coach Chan Gailey to coach the team. He had a long way to go to get the Bills back to their glory days in the early 1990s.

BILLS QUARTERBACK DOUG FLUTIE PASSES THE BALL DURING A 1999 AFC WILD-CARD PLAYOFF GAME AGAINST THE MIAMI DOLPHINS.

TIMELINE

1959 The Buffalo Bills and Boston Patriots join six charter members preparing for the first season of the American Football League.

1960 Buffalo loses its first game 27–3 to the New York Titans.

1964 The Bills beat the San Diego Chargers 20–7 in the AFL Championship Game.

1965 The Bills shut out the San Diego Chargers 23–0 to repeat as AFL champion.

1967 Buffalo loses to Kansas City 31–7 in the AFL Championship Game on January 1, missing a chance to play in the first Super Bowl.

1970 The Bills and nine other AFL franchises merge into the NFL.

1973 Bills running back O. J. Simpson becomes the first in NFL history to rush for more than 2,000 yards in a season.

1986 Marv Levy takes over as head coach of the Bills.

1990 The Bills start a streak of 10 straight wins in AFC playoff games.

1991 The New York Giants edge Buffalo 20–19 on January 27 in Super Bowl XXV.

1992	The Washington Redskins beat the Bills 37–24 on January 26 in Super Bowl XXVI.
1993	The Bills produce the biggest comeback in NFL playoff history in January, rallying from 35–3 to defeat the Houston Oilers 41–38 in overtime.
1993	The Dallas Cowboys pound the Bills 52–17 on January 31 in Super Bowl XXVII.
1994	Dallas beats Buffalo 30–13 on January 30 in Super Bowl XXVIII.
1995	The Bills win the last of their 10 straight AFC playoff games with a 37–22 win over the Miami Dolphins on December 30.
1999	Buffalo qualifies for the playoffs for the tenth time in 12 years.
2000	The "Music City Miracle," a 75-yard kickoff return with the help of a lateral, allows Tennessee to pull out a 22–16 playoff victory over the Bills on January 8.
2000	The Bills begin a streak of 10 years without a playoff appearance.
2010	The Bills hire Chan Gailey as head coach.

QUICK STATS

FRANCHISE HISTORY

1960–69 (AFL)
1970– (NFL)

SUPER BOWLS
(wins in bold)

1990 (XXV), **1991 (XXVI)**,
1992 (XXVII), 1993 (XXVIII)

AFL CHAMPIONSHIP GAMES
(1960–69)

1964, **1965**, 1966

AFC CHAMPIONSHIP GAMES
(since 1970 AFL-NFL merger)

1988, 1990, 1991, 1992, 1993

DIVISION CHAMPIONSHIPS
(since 1970 AFL-NFL merger)

1980, 1988, 1989, 1990, 1991, 1993,
1995

KEY PLAYERS
(position, seasons with team)

Joe DeLamielleure (G, 1973–79,
   1985)
Jim Kelly (QB, 1986–96)
Jack Kemp (QB, 1962–69)
Reggie McKenzie (G, 1972–82)
Eric Moulds (WR, 1996–2005)
Andre Reed (WR, 1985–99)
Billy Shaw (G, 1961–69)
O. J. Simpson (RB, 1969–77)
Bruce Smith (DE, 1985–99)
Thurman Thomas (RB, 1988–99)

KEY COACHES

Marv Levy (1986–97): 112–70;
   11–8 (playoffs)
Lou Saban (1962–65, 1972–76):
   68–45–4; 2–2 (playoffs)

HOME FIELDS

Ralph Wilson Stadium (1973–)
   Known as Rich Stadium 1973–98
War Memorial Stadium (1960–72)

*All statistics through 2009 season

QUOTES AND ANECDOTES

Buffalo Bills running back Thurman Thomas missed the opening possession of Super Bowl XXVI when he misplaced his helmet. The Bills lost to the Washington Redskins 37–24.

Linebacker Mike Stratton was one of the defensive leaders when the Bills won their two AFL Championships. Had the Super Bowl been created two years earlier, Buffalo would have faced off against the NFL champion Cleveland Browns in 1964. They would have faced the NFL champion Green Bay Packers in 1965. Had that been the case, Stratton believed Buffalo would have won a Super Bowl. "I would have relished the opportunity," Stratton told *USA Today* in 2009. "And, I would have picked us."

During his lengthy career in sports, Lou Saban also served as president of the New York Yankees baseball team. "He has been my friend and mentor for over 50 years, and one of the people who helped shape my life," said Yankees owner George Steinbrenner. He brought Saban to the Yankees for the 1981 and 1982 seasons. Steinbrenner had coached wide receivers on Saban's staff at Northwestern University in 1955. Saban died in 2009. He was 87.

The Buffalo Bills' Wall of Fame was started in 1980 to honor former players, administrators, and coaches who played significant roles in team history. The Wall of Fame includes: Eddie Abramoski, Joe DeLamielleure, Elbert Dubenion, Joe Ferguson, Kent Hull, Robert James, Bob Kalsu, Jim Kelly, Jack Kemp, Marv Levy, Patrick J. McGroder, George Saimes, Tom Sestak, Billy Shaw, O. J. Simpson, Fred Smerlas, Mike Stratton, Darryl Talley, Ralph Wilson, and "The 12th Man." The 12th Man refers to the team's fans.

GLOSSARY

comeback

Coming from behind to take a lead in a particular game.

contender

A team that is considered good enough to win a championship.

draft

A system used by professional sports leagues to select new players in order to spread incoming talent among all teams.

expansion

The addition of new units to an existing entity, as in the case of new teams being added to a sports league.

franchise

An entire sports organization, including the players, coaches, and staff.

hall of fame

A place built to honor noteworthy achievements by athletes in their respective sports.

lateral

To pass the ball sideways or backward.

merge

To unite into a single body.

retire

To officially end one's career.

rookie

A first-year professional athlete.

waivers

The process of making a player available to other teams in the league.

wild card

Playoff berths given to the best remaining teams that did not win their respective divisions.

FOR MORE INFORMATION

Further Reading

Gruver, Ed. *The American Football League: A Year-By-Year History, 1960–1969*. Jefferson, NC: McFarland & Company, 1998.

Miller, Jeffrey. *Game Changers: The Greatest Plays in Buffalo Bills Football History*. Chicago, IL: Triumph, 2009.

Miller, Jeffrey. *Rockin' the Rockpile: The Buffalo Bills and the American Football League*. Toronto, ON: ECW Press, 2007.

Web Links

To learn more about the Buffalo Bills, visit ABDO Publishing Company online at **www.abdopublishing.com**. Web sites about the Bills are featured on our Book Links page. These links are routinely monitored and updated to provide the most current information available.

Places to Visit

Pro Football Hall of Fame
2121 George Halas Drive Northwest
Canton, OH 44708
330-456-8207
www.profootballhof.com
This hall of fame and museum highlights the greatest players and moments in the history of the National Football League. Eight people affiliated with the Buffalo Bills are enshrined there. They include Jim Kelly and owner Ralph Wilson Jr.

Ralph Wilson Stadium
1 Bills Drive
Orchard Park, NY 14127
716-648-1800
www.buffalobills.com/tickets/stadium/maps.html
The suburban Buffalo stadium is the site of Bills home games. The stadium opened in 1973.

St. John Fisher College
3690 East Avenue
Rochester, NY 14618
585-385-8000
www.buffalobills.com/team/training-camp/index.html
The home of the Buffalo Bills' training camp. Fans may visit training camp on any day of the week to watch. Admission is free.

INDEX

About the Author

Tom Robinson is a sports writer and an author and editor of educational books. The Clarks Summit, Pennsylvania, resident has covered National Football League games and issues during three decades of writing about sports. He has written more than 20 books for young readers.